DELEGATING FOR RESULTS

DELEGATING FOR RESULTS

Robert B Maddux

KOGAN
PAGE

Copyright © Crisp Publications Inc 1990

First published in the United States of America in 1990 by Crisp Publications Inc, 95 First Street, Los Altos, California 94022, USA.

This edition first published in Great Britain in 1990 by Kogan Page Ltd, 120 Pentonville Road, London N1 9JN

British Library Cataloguing in Publication Data

A CIP record for this book is available from the British Library.

ISBN 0-7494-315-2
ISBN 0-7494-316-0 Pbk

Typeset by the Castlefield Press, Wellingborough, Northants.
Printed and bound in Great Britain by
Biddles Limited, Guildford.

Contents

Preface

One of the most difficult tasks for supervisors, especially new ones, is learning to apportion the work among the employees they supervise. The difficulty is often due to just those personal qualities – job knowledge, competent personal performance, initiative, motivation and a reasonable degree of interpersonal skills – that made them successful employees in the first place and ultimately led to their promotion. Those qualities might lead new supervisors to believe they can do all the important work in their unit by themselves.

These qualities may have made the employee successful in the past, but they can become a heavy burden if they are misapplied in the supervisory role. The new supervisor must contrast the old assignment with the new, and identify the critical differences. One of the most important differences is this: since the new task is too much for one person to accomplish, other employees have been assigned to help. Those employees bring skills and knowledge in varying degrees and expect to use and develop them. So the supervisor is responsible not only for his or her performance, but also for the performance and development of his or her subordinates. Their combined efforts are required to accomplish the goals and objectives of the unit.

The supervisor must recognise the role change from performing tasks to managing the performance of others. Concentration must now focus on planning, organising, motivating and controlling. This requires learning new skills and backing away from doing tasks that can be done by subordinates. The supervisor must learn to delegate and do it well.

If the skills of delegation are not learned and polished at every opportunity, success will be limited and the likelihood of promotion will be low. Those with limited delegation skills who are promoted will find their new jobs extremely difficult, and they will ultimately have a negative impact on the productivity of their unit.

Delegation is not some mysterious art available to only a chosen few. It is a basic management process that can be learned and honed to a fine edge by anyone who is willing to make the effort and able to get some practice. Providing the principles is what this book is about. Applying them is up to you. Good luck!

Robert B Maddux

CHAPTER 1
The Role of the Manager

Management is a process

When a person assumes a managerial position there is a distinct change in that person's relationships with other employees, and a new set of tasks begins to unfold. These tasks, taken together, are generally referred to as the management process. Management practitioners and scholars vary widely in their definitions of this process. These differences are usually nothing more than a choice of words. Some consolidate similar functions into broad categories – others prefer an extensive listing of individual functions.

The management process for our purposes consists of four main functions. These are: planning, organising, motivating and controlling. Good delegation requires skill in all four!

PLANNING   ORGANISING

Determining objectives and setting goals; drawing up plans that will implement these goals	Assessing resources (needed and available); scheduling work distribution; drawing up flow charts
Setting standards and checkpoints for evaluating work against these standards; sampling the work-flow; collecting feedback	Supervising the workers; training and developing them; giving orders; maintaining motivation and a productive work environment

CONTROLLING   MOTIVATING

Planning

Planning is the thinking that precedes doing. It is concerned with setting goals and objectives for an organisational unit and with preparing plans and schedules to accomplish them. In the list below, tick those statements that you consider important elements in planning.

☐ 1. Interpreting goals and objectives passed down from above as the result of planning performed at a higher level.

☐ 2. Gathering the thoughts and ideas of the employees who are directly involved, as well as your own thoughts and ideas.

☐ 3. Formulating and issuing policies and procedures to accomplish goals and objectives.

☐ 4. Examining alternatives and selecting the activities and programmes that will lead to successful results.

☐ 5. Establishing timetables and completion targets in keeping with priorities.

☐ 6. Determining standards of performance and how results will be measured.

☐ 7. Identifying the resources necessary for task accomplishment – people, time, money, material – and determining their availability.

If you are an effective planner, you ticked all the above.

Organising

Once planning is underway, organising becomes essential. Resources – people, capital, equipment, raw materials, facilities – must be brought together in the most productive way to accomplish goals and objectives. In the list below, tick the items that you think organising should provide.

☐ 1. Appropriate staffing – the right number of people with the essential skills to perform the work that has to be done.

☐ 2. Delineation of responsibility and authority.

☐ 3. Alignment of major functions and structuring of the component parts into effective work units and teams.

☐ 4. Manuals, administrative guides, and other tools to show how responsibility has been assigned and authority delegated.

☐ 5. A communications system for reporting and co-ordination between people and organisations.

☐ 6. Methods of problem solving and conflict resolution.

☐ 7. Facilities and equipment needed for task accomplishment.

If you ticked all seven boxes, give yourself top marks for organisation.

Motivating

Motivation, along with planning and organising, plays an important part in the level of performance that will be achieved in any endeavour. To check your views on motivation, review the following statements and indicate which are true and which are false.

True	False	
_____	_____	1. The needs and desires of employees have little bearing on motivation.
_____	_____	2. It is important to create an environment in which employees can meet their needs while meeting the needs of the organisation.
_____	_____	3. Results generally improve when people are able to participate in deciding what the results should be.
_____	_____	4. Motivation to achieve results is improved when employees are recognised for their contributions.
_____	_____	5. Studies have shown that communication has very little to do with motivation.
_____	_____	6. Coaching and training tend to raise personal levels of motivation.
_____	_____	7. Motivation to achieve results usually increases as employees are given authority to make decisions affecting those results.
_____	_____	8. Good supervisors pay close attention to the way employees respond when they assign work.

Statements 2,3,4,6,7 and 8 are true.

Controlling

Controlling is concerned with results. It involves follow-up to compare results with plans and to make adjustments where results differ from expectations. In the following list of statements about controlling, identify those you believe to be true and those you believe to be false.

Controlling requires:

True   False

_____ _____ 1. Devising ways to assess whether goals,
                  objectives, or standards have been met in
                  a timely and cost-effective manner.

_____ _____ 2. Punishing employees who have missed
                  their targets.

_____ _____ 3. Formulating methods by which the use of
                  various resources can be measured and
                  evaluated for future planning puposes.

_____ _____ 4. Establishing systems that provide feedback
                  at key points as the work progresses, so
                  that deviations from the plan can be
                  identified, evaluated and acted upon.

_____ _____ 5. Limiting employee authority to minor
                  details.

_____ _____ 6. Reporting the status of activities and
                  projects to those who need to know.

> Statements 2 and 5 are false.

How work gets done in organisations

Management is a leadership effort to integrate and to use a
variety of resources effectively to accomplish an objective. It
applies to all organisations, whether they are private
businesses, hospitals or part of the Civil Service. Managers
will do well to remember there is no one best way to plan,
organise, motivate or control. Each manager must continually
increase his or her knowledge of management concepts and
draw upon them until a winning combination is found that
fits him or her, the people supervised, and the work involved.

One factor is central, however, to every management task. That factor is **delegation.** The manager must know what is expected of his or her unit, when it is expected, and how best to employ his or her human resources to obtain the desired results. This means assigning work in a planned and thoughtful way.

Delegation is giving people things to do. Management is accomplishing organisational goals by working through individuals and groups. It is easy to see that the two are closely entwined. And it is obvious that the manager who is not delegating is not managing.

Delegation, of all the skills and activities of a manager, is one of the most indispensable.

Case Study 1
The do-it–yourself manager

Joanne was a capable and enthusiastic professional. She was promoted to manage a group of five professionals doing work that was very similar to her own previous assignment.

She began in her new position thinking, 'I was promoted because of my excellent performance in past assignments. Therefore, I must have greater expertise than any of my subordinates and can probably do most of the work better and faster than they can. I will train them when I have time, but right now I had better concentrate on getting the work out.'

Joanne did not pass on any major areas of responsibility to her employees; she did the work herself. As time passed, her hours of work increased steadily and she was less and less available to her peers – and to her own supervisor, with whom coordination was important. Her employees were given only the most routine work, received no training, and actually knew very little about the major projects that were in progress. One actually resigned because of the lack of challenge and personal growth. Joanne was too busy to replace him.

Finally, after 60 days, Joanne's supervisor called her in to discuss her performance. What would you have said to Joanne if you had been her supervisor? Please summarise your comments below, then compare them with the author's on page 68.

_____

_____

_____

_____

Technical, human and conceptual skills

Many new supervisors and managers approach their jobs much like Joanne, and fall into the same trap. They do not see the difference between technical, human and conceptual skills, and how these skills apply to their position. Think of them this way.

DEFINITIONS		
Technical skills	**Human skills**	**Conceptual skills**
Ability to use knowledge, methods and equipment to perform specific tasks; acquired from experience and training.	Ability and judgement in working with people, including an understanding of motivation and leadership.	Ability to understand the complexities of the overall organisation and where one's own unit fits into the total picture.

Lower level supervisors need considerable technical skill because they are often required to train and develop new employees and technicians. At the other extreme, senior managers do not need to know how to perform all the specific tasks at the operational level, but they should understand how all the functions are interrelated. The common denominator that is crucial at all levels is human skill.

As supervisors move up in management they must learn to delegate jobs requiring technical skill to their subordinates, to give themselves time to learn the human and conceptual skills now required of them.

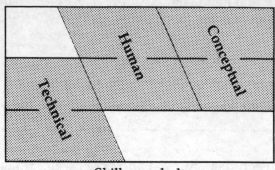

Skills needed

What can delegating do for me?

New managers, like Joanne, often assign a low priority to delegation because they are unsure of how to go about it and don't see the benefits. Some actually think delegation is more trouble than it's worth. A number of advantages of good delegation are listed below. Tick those you would like to achieve.

☐ 1. More work can be accomplished and deadlines can be met more easily.

☐ 2. Employees become involved and committed.

☐ 3. The assignment of specific responsibility and authority makes control less difficult.

☐ 4. Employees grow and develop.

☐ 5. Human resources are utilised more fully and productivity improves.

☐ 6. Individual performance can be measured more accurately.

☐ 8. Compensation, including bonuses, can be more directly related to individual performance.

☐   8. A diversity of products, operations and people can be managed effectively.

☐   9. Distant operations can be managed with less travel and stress.

☐ 10. Employee satisfaction and recognition are enhanced.

☐ 11. The manager has time for planning, organising, motivating and controlling.

☐ 12. The manager is freed to do those tasks only he or she can do.

Please add any other advantages you can think of in the spaces below.

☐ 13. _____

☐ 14. _____

☐ 15. _____

CHAPTER 2

Analysing Personal Delegation Skills

How well do I delegate?

Here is an opportunity to learn how well you delegate. This scale will help identify your strengths and determine where improvement would be beneficial. Circle the number that best describes you. The higher the number, the more the statement describes you. When you have finished, add up the numbers circled and put the total in the space provided.

1. Each of my employees knows what
   I expect of her or him.   7 6 5 4 3 2 1

2. I involve employees in goal-setting,
   problem-solving and productivity
   improvement activities.   7 6 5 4 3 2 1

3. I place my personal emphasis on
   planning, organising, motivating
   and controlling, rather than doing
   tasks others could do.   7 6 5 4 3 2 1

4. When assigning work, I select the
   assignee thoughtfully.   7 6 5 4 3 2 1

5. When a problem occurs on a project
   I have delegated, I give the employee
   a reasonable chance to work it out for
   him/herself.   7 6 5 4 3 2 1

6. When I delegate work to
   employees, I brief them fully on
   the details with which I am familiar   7 6 5 4 3 2 1

7. I see delegation as one way to help
   employees develop their skills,
   and I assign work accordingly.   7 6 5 4 3 2 1

8. I support and help employees in
   emergencies, but I do not permit
   them to leave work for me to do.   7 6 5 4 3 2 1

9. When I assign work, I stress the
   results desired, rather than how
   to accomplish them.   7 6 5 4 3 2 1

10. When I delegate a project, I make
    sure everyone concerned knows
    who is in charge.   7 6 5 4 3 2 1

11. When delegating work, I balance
    authority with need and experience. 7 6 5 4 3 2 1

12. I hold my employees responsible
    for results.   7 6 5 4 3 2 1

TOTAL _____

A score between 72 and 84 suggests you are on target. A score between 48 and 71 indicates you are getting by, but could improve. Anything below 48 means you need to make changes.

Symptoms of poor delegation

There are many symptoms of poor delegation. They can usually be seen in the work habits of the manager, the attitude of the employees, or the productivity of the group. In the list below, tick the symptoms that are found in your organisation.

☐ Deadlines are frequently missed.

☐ Some employees are much busier than others.

☐ The supervisor (me) is usually too busy to talk to employees.

☐ Employees are unsure of their authority.

☐ No one in the group is ever ready for promotion.

☐ Employee decisions are often overruled.

☐ No one seems to know who is in charge of a project.

☐ The organisation is plagued by slow decision making.

☐ The supervisor (me) never has time to visit employee work areas.

☐ Changes in plans and objectives are not passed on to the employees who need to know about them.

☐ Employees are assigned tasks they can't handle without training.

☐ The supervisor (me) sometimes intervenes in a project or assignment without informing the delegatee.

☐ Employees frequently request transfers to other groups.

☐ The communications flow is sporadic, incomplete and often too late.

☐ The supervisor (me) often takes work home and sometimes reschedules his or her holiday because of the work-load.

☐ Talented employees are bored.

☐ The supervisor (me) insists all mail must first pass through his or her office.

If you ticked more than one or two of the above statements, you should look carefully at your delegation practices and ask yourself why these conditions exist.

Common barriers to delegation

Ineffective delegators rationalise their inadequacies in various ways. They usually centre around obstacles (natural or self-made) in themselves, in the characteristics of their employees, or in the situation itself. In the following list of attitudes, indicate those that affect your delegation practices by ticking 'Yes'. If they do not affect you, tick 'No'. Think about each statement carefully and be totally honest.

Yes	No	Self-imposed obstacles
_____	_____	I prefer performing operating tasks – not management functions – because I understand them better and I know how.
_____	_____	I can do the work better than anyone else.
_____	_____	I don't know how to delegate.
_____	_____	My employees won't like me if I expect too much of them.
_____	_____	I am not certain to whom I should delegate.
_____	_____	It is easier and quicker to do things myself.
_____	_____	We just can't afford to make any mistakes.

Yes	No	Employee-imposed obstacles
_____	_____	My employees lack experience and competence.
_____	_____	My employees are already overloaded.
_____	_____	My employees resist responsibility.
_____	_____	My employees fear criticism and avoid risk.

Situation-imposed obstacles

_____	_____	Management expects me to handle the really important tasks personally.
_____	_____	My employees can't be trusted to work on their own.
_____	_____	We are seriously understaffed. I have no one to whom I can delegate.
_____	_____	Most of our decisions are made under crisis conditions.

If you answered yes to any of the above, you will find this book most helpful.

Fact versus fallacy

The statements above to which you answered 'Yes' need to be examined objectively. They usually are invalid and keep supervisors from delegating as they should. Several of them deserve close scrutiny.

The fallacy of omnipotence

This is the 'I can do it better myself' syndrome. Even if it is true, the choice is not between the quality of the supervisor's work on a given task and that of the employee. The choice is between the benefits of the supervisor's performance on a single task versus the benefits of spending his or her time in planning, organising, motivating, controlling, and developing an effective team. The team will eventually outperform the manager and continue to grow.

The fear of being disliked

Though few managers will admit it, most are concerned that their employees will dislike or resent them if they press a lot of work on them. Such managers will risk personal burnout rather than inconvenience an employee.

Interestingly enough, employees rate supervisors who make full use of delegation good or excellent. Poor delegators receive low ratings.

Lack of confidence in employees

Managers who lack confidence in their employees should look to themselves for the answer. They are, or should be, in control of the situation.

If employees cannot handle delegated assignments, the manager has either hired incompetent people, failed to provide them with appropriate training, or has not made the effort to find out the extent of their capabilities. The remedy: identify strengths and weaknesses, and train or replace those who still cannot meet the required standards.

Employees expect the answers from me

This is usually how managers rationalise taking problem solving and decision making away from employees. It occurs when an employee brings a problem to a supervisor who says, 'Why don't you leave it with me and I'll get back to you.' When the supervisor does get back to the employee it is with the solution. The employee only wanted to talk about the problem – they did not want to be given the answer.

I can do it faster than I can explain it

A supervisor who uses this excuse to justify doing an operating task that he or she likes but someone else could be taught to do, is making a serious mistake. If he or she doesn't take the time to teach someone else to do the task, they will still be performing it far into the future. This consumes valuable time and effort that could be better spent on tasks only the supervisor can do.

Sometimes a supervisor truly cannot delegate. But as the chart below demonstrates, upward progression requires more and more delegating and less 'doing'.

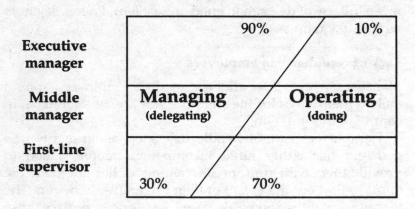

CHAPTER 3
Preparing to Delegate

Analyse your job

To become an effective delegator, you must have your own job well in hand. This means periodically:

- Reviewing your duties and responsibilities as a manager. How have they changed? What new things do you have to learn? How do they affect your unit? What are the new challenges? What old practices need to be stopped?

- Reaffirming the primary objectives of your unit. Have there been any changes that affect priorities or need to be communicated to employees?

- Highlighting the key results areas. What are the make or break factors in your assignment? What are the areas in which specific results are essential?

- Re-examining your work-load to identify those few tasks only you can do.

Remember, you are a manager, not an individual contributor. Your job is to utilise your human resources effectively to accomplish organisational goals. You must sort out the important from the unimportant and proceed on a priority basis. The more you develop your employees, and the more you delegate to them, the more they can help you identify key results areas and meet objectives. Let go of tasks that rightfully belong to your employees. That includes trouble shooting and problem solving in their areas of responsibility. Certainly, see that they are properly trained and help them when they flounder, but be sure to give them a chance to do the job for which they were employed.

Decide what to delegate

> Any time you perform a task someone else could do, you keep yourself from a task only you can do.

Managers usually delegate to give themselves more time to do complex and difficult management tasks, to improve productivity, or to develop their employees. Some types of work you should consider delegating are listed below.

Decisions you make most frequently Minor decisions and repetitive routines often consume a large part of the day. Most, if not all, of these can be delegated by teaching employees the policies and procedures that apply. They probably already know the details better than you.

List two possibilities:

1. _____

2. _____

Functions that you are expert in

These are usually operating tasks rather than management functions. Your challenge as a manager is to motivate others to produce better results than you ever did as an individual performer. Part of the time you save can be used to learn about other functions so that you can manage them better.

List two possibilities:

1. _____

2. _____

Tasks and projects for which you are least qualified

It is almost certain that some of your employees are better qualified and can do parts of the job better than you. Let them.

List two possibilities:

1. _____

2. _____

Functions you dislike

Performings functions we dislike is distasteful, and we often put them off or do them poorly. Examine the likes and dislikes of your staff as well as their talents. You will nearly always find someone who likes the job and can do it well. If they need training, provide it.

27

List two possibilities:

1. _____

2. _____

Work that will provide experience for employees	This makes growth in the present job a reality and helps keep employees challenged and motivated.

List two possibilities:

1. _____

2. _____

Assignments that will add variety to routine work	A change of pace is usually welcome and is often a good way to motivate an employee whose job is growing dull.

List two possibilities:

1. _____

2. _____

Activities that will make a position more complete	As employees become more proficient, they often have time to spare. Add complementary duties and responsibilities to give their positions more substance.

List two possibilities:

1. _____

2. _____

Tasks that will increase the number of people who can perform critical assignments

Maximise the strength of the group by giving people the necessary experience to back one another up during emergencies or periods of unusually heavy work.

List two possibilities:

1. _____

2. _____

Opportunities to use and reinforce creative talents

Employees are not creative in a stifling environment. They must be given a certain amount of freedom and the opportunity to show initiative. Stimulate them with difficult problems and projects, and reward creative solutions.

List two possibilities:

1. _____

2. _____

Case Study 2
Baffled by the budget

Jack is an excellent manager of manufacturing, but he has just learned in a performance review that he may have a fatal flaw. He is always over budget and his explanations are usually weak and late. This happens even though he prepares the budget himself, and personally maintains what appear to be adequate controls. Now his supervisor has given him an ultimatum: 'Get control over your budget or I will have to demote you to a less responsible position.'

Jack's administrative assistant, who has an excellent accounting background, expertise with computers and some experience with budgets, would like to help. So would his section heads, who believe the budget would be more representative of reality if they had some input. Jack, however, feels it is his responsibility and he has to do it himself.

In the space below, outline what you would suggest that Jack should do to correct this problem. Then compare your answer with the author's suggestions on page 69.

My suggestions:

_____

_____

_____

_____

_____

Planning the delegation

Deciding what to delegate is only the first step in the delegation process. Delegation, like most other management tasks, is most successful when it's planned. It may take a few minutes, for simple tasks; or a few hours, when the project is complex. Your planning should include at least the following considerations. In the checklist below, tick 'Yes' if you include the item in your planning; tick 'No' if you do not.

Yes	No	
____	____	1. What is the objective to be accomplished?
____	____	2. What are the critical completion dates?
____	____	3. What standards will have to be met?
____	____	4. What decisions will have to be made?
____	____	5. How much authority can I delegate?
____	____	6. How much authority will I delegate?
____	____	7. What instructions or orders will the person(s) be authorised to issue?
____	____	8. Does a budget need to be developed or followed?
____	____	9. Who will the person(s) need to interface with in my group? In other units?
____	____	10. What information do I need to give?
____	____	11. How much do I want to be involved?
____	____	12. What feedback do I want and when do I want it?
____	____	13. Who will I need to keep informed of progress?
____	____	14. Do I need to tell others who is in charge?
____	____	15. To whom should I delegate?

If you ticked 'No' for any of the above items, plan to change your delegation behaviour so that you can tick them 'Yes' in the future.

Task/project analysis planning sheet

Key results areas	Results expected	Critical deadlines

This planning sheet, plus the checklist on page 31, will help you to plan your next delegation more effectively.

Standards to be met	Budget	Critical interfaces	Frequency of feedback

CHAPTER 4

Selecting the Right Person

Making choices

As soon as you have completed your delegation plan, identify the appropriate person to perform the task. Some of the many things to consider are listed below.

Does the work belong to a particular position?

Some tasks or projects fit neatly into existing work assignments and can be logically delegated there.

List two examples from the past or two possibilities for the future:

1. _____

2. _____

Who has the interest and/or the ability?

Analyse employee job performance periodically, and keep an inventory of the interests and abilities of your staff. Look for opportunities to give employees who are attending classes a chance to apply what they are learning.

Give consideration to interest as well as ability. A minimally qualified person may take the assignment enthusiastically and develop the required skills; the best-qualified person with a low level of interest may do a poor job.

List two examples from the past or two prospects for the future:

1. _____

2. _____

Who will find the work challenging?

Studies reflect that large numbers of employees are unchallenged by their work, and that their boredom is reflected in their performance. Give them the pleasure of a new opportunity to achieve.

List two prospects for the future:

1. _____

2. _____

Who will the assignment stretch and help to grow?

Some employees thrive on challenge and are willing to develop new skills to meet new job requirements. Give them the opportunity.

Identify two people in this category:

1. _____

2. _____

Who has been overlooked when you have delegated in the past?

Delegate to all of your employees and stretch them when you can. Avoid favouritism or overburdening some members of your staff. Delegating to an employee who has been untested in the past requires careful planning, but the pay-off in added performance is potentially high.

An assignment delegated with care can bring a problem employee up to standard. An employee with unused potential can be motivated to new heights of achievement.

Every time you give an 'unknown' the chance to perform in a new way, the overall depth, versatility and morale of your unit will improve.

List two possibilities for the future:

1. _____

2. _____

Who has the time?

If an employee has occasional periods with a light work-load, look for opportunities to use that employee's time productively.

List two possibilities:

1. _____

2. _____

Who is being prepared for a new assignment or promotion?	Employees being prepared for a new assignment or promotion often profit from delegated assignments that relate to their new duties and responsibilities.

List two possibilities:

1. _____

2. _____

You really do not know what people can do until you give them a chance under the proper conditions.

Making the pre-delegation assessment

The planning phase prior to assigning work is the manager's opportunity to organise the distribution of work and to schedule it within his or her unit. The quality of your preparations will largely determine the success of the delegation. Managers who ignore the planning are usually those who are keeping far too much work to themselves, or those who indiscriminately dump assignments on staff members. Asking yourself the following questions in advance will help you make better delegation decisions:

1. What work needs to be done?

2. What can and should be delegated?

3. What is the best match of work with individual employee abilities and interests?

4. Who would the assignment help develop?

5. Who can do it for me now?

6. Who can be trained to do it?

7. What is the employee's current work-load and level of performance?

8. What is my best course of action, other than doing it myself, given the time constraints involved?

The chart on page 40 is a good place to summarise and record your thoughts.

Remember your secretary's potential

Managers with secretaries, or administrative assistants, often fail to delegate properly to them. They see them only as someone to do word processing, answer the telephones, and keep up the files. This is a major mistake.

When secretaries have been properly trained and participate actively in the management of their supervisor's business affairs, they can be of incalculable value in a number of areas. Consider the following possibilities. As you do, check the tasks you already delegate to your secretary or administrative assistant, and be alert to new ways to enrich their jobs and facilitate your own.

☐ 1. Screening and directing mail to the proper person for action.

☐ 2. Composing correspondence for your signature.

☐ 3. Organising your time, coordinating appointments and assuring deadlines are met.

☐ 4. Following up on reports and other work on which you, or others, have set a due date, and reporting their status to you.

☐ 5. Coordinating conference calls.

☐ 6. Organising and setting up meetings on your behalf.

☐ 7. Gathering information needed for decision making.

☐ 8. Maintaining appropriate personal records and files.

☐ 9. Redirecting telephone calls and correspondence that come to you, but that should go elsewhere.

☐ 10. Performing basic research on projects you have retained for yourself.

☐ 11. Maintaining confidential records.

☐ 12. Facilitating communication through your office in your absence.

Add other possibilities that fit your situation.

☐ 13. _____

☐ 14. _____

☐ 15. _____

Case Study 3
Making choices

Susan has been in her new managerial assignment for approximately two months. She is trying to make the transition from being an outstanding individual performer to an effective manager. Delegation is very difficult for her, but she is making a real effort to learn to do it well. She directs a group of eight.

Her supervisor asked her recently how she was getting on with her delegation efforts. Susan replied, 'I think I am doing pretty well. I have learned that Mary Wong is very knowledgeable about all aspects of the work, and she always completes the assignments I give her on time – even if she has

Delegation log

Key results areas	Results expected	Who can do it for me now

Who can be trained to do it	Assigned to	Follow-up required

to work overtime and at weekends. So I give her all the big jobs and let the others stick to the routines they know best. My other employees just aren't qualified to carry the burden that Mary does.'

If you were Susan's supervisor, how would you respond?

_____

_____

_____

_____

_____

_____

_____

_____

_____

_____

Check your answer with the author's on page 69

CHAPTER 5

Making the Delegation

Communicating the delegation

Face-to-face, two-way discussion is the critical step that should end with the employee's commitment and the supervisor's assurance that the results needed will be achieved.

Delegation is not just pushing work down. When you are delegating, you are consulting and developing as well as assigning work. Open communication is vital, and success depends ultimately on the communication skills of the manager and the employee, and on the quality of their relationship. When there is a lack of trust on either side, or poor communication between them, the necessary understanding and motivation is unlikely to be there.

The following steps are essential in communicating an assignment:

1. *Describe as fully as possible the project or task and the results expected.*

   Pass on all the information needed to get the job started, or let the employee know where it can be obtained. Indicate who else will be involved and describe their roles.

2. *Agree on standards of performance and timetables.*

   The scope of the assignment has already been determined, but you will want the employee's input on standards and a reasonable timetable for completion of the assignment.

3. *Determine any training or special help that will be needed, and when it will be provided.*

4. *Define parameters and the resources, including budget, that will be available.*

5. *State the amount and frequency of feedback you expect.*

6. *Spell out the amount of authority being delegated.*

This should be balanced according to the complexity of the task, your confidence in the employee, and your need to keep others informed.

See page 46 for selection of appropriate level.

7. *Tell others who is in charge.*

It is important you do not become a communications block between the delegatee and others who will be involved or affected.

It is easy to see from these seven basic points that delegation is *not* more trouble than it's worth. Have you been missing some good opportunities because you thought it was?

Missed opportunities

Supervisors who find themselves deeply involved in the detailed work of their units sometimes wake up to the fact that the job is controlling them. They are controlling nothing. If they examine the situation carefully (while pondering the fact that their employees went home hours ago and they are still working), they often see the reason for their plight. Their reaction is usually, 'If I had delegated this to David or Sue in the first place, I wouldn't be having this problem now.'

How many times have you missed the opportunity to delegate, or thought you had, and found yourself doing work someone else could and should have done?

By now, some missed opportunities to delegate have no

doubt come to mind. List them in the space provided below ... and resolve not to let it happen again.

My missed opportunities

_____

_____

_____

_____

_____

_____

_____

_____

_____

_____

_____

Six levels of authority

A common management mistake is failing to delegate the amount of authority that is appropriate to the task, the surrounding circumstances, and the employee's ability. Some managers do not delegate any authority because they want full personal control. Others give full authority because they want to be free of the task. Most of the time, something in between these two extremes is called for. Before you make your next delegation, review the authority levels described on the next page and select one that fits your needs.

Level of authority	Assignment	Reason
1	Look into the situation. Get all the facts and report them to me. I'll decide what to do.	The employee is new to the job and the supervisor wants to retain control of the outcome.
2	Identify the problem. Determine alternative solutions and the pluses and minuses of each. Recommend one for my approval.	The employee is being developed and the supervisor wants to see how he or she approaches problems and makes decisions.
3	Examine the issues. Let me know what you intend to do, but don't take action until you check.	The supervisor has confidence in the employee, but does not want action taken without his or her approval This may be because of constraints from higher management, or the need to communicate the action to others before it is taken.
4	Solve the problem. Let me know what you intend to do, then do it, unless I say no.	The supervisor has respect for the employee's ability and judgement, and only wants a final check before action is taken.
5	Take action on this matter, and let me know what you did.	The supervisor has full confidence in the employee and has no need to be consulted before action is taken. He or she only wants to know the outcome.
6	Take action. No further contact with me is necessary.	The supervisor has total confidence in the employee. The employee has full authority to act and does not need to report the results back to the supervisor.

Following through

It is important, however, that the manager follows through with any support, resources or information that have been promised. It is also important that a feedback mechanism, suitable to the situation, is established between the employee assigned the task and the manager. These considerations are all part of the preparations for delegation, and should be covered when the delegation is made.

THE ESSENTIAL ELEMENTS OF FOLLOW-THROUGH		
The manager's role	The manager's communication	The manager's action
Encourage independence.	Share all pertinent information.	Assess results.
Allow freedom of action in keeping with the level of delegation.	Do not become a communications block between the employee and the others involved.	Suggest corrective action if appropriate and unrecognised by the those handling tasks.
Support initiative and creativity.		Help solve problems, but only those beyond the employee's ability to handle.
Share opinions and show interest.	Monitor progress, but do not hover.	
Accept mistakes and learn from them.	Provide honest feedback.	Evaluate performance.
Provide training when needed.	Insist that your need for information on progress is fulfilled on time.	Plan any needed training for the future.
Live with differences as long as objectives are met.		Compliment efforts and reward success.
Be available.		
Don't take the job back unless absolutely essential (coach through problems).		

Case Study 4
The incomplete data dilemma

Kate is the manager of an insurance company claims group. Her employees are well trained and have considerable experience in claims work. Much of the work is routine, but occasionally an unusual claim is submitted that requires a great deal of investigation. When this occurs, Kate assigns one of her claims representatives to the case. She delegates the authority necessary for that person to gather the facts, develop alternative solutions and recommend the action to be taken. However, something always seems to go wrong. Key information is lacking or has not been considered. This is true even though Kate often acts as the point of contact when people outside the company are providing pertinent data. She always tries to pass this information on quickly and in a form that those handling the assignment will understand.

She has had several discussions with her staff about this, but these have only resulted in their becoming angry and defensive.

What do you think the problem is? Jot down your ideas in the space below.

_____

_____

_____

_____

_____

_____

_____

_____

Turn to page 70 and compare your ideas with those of the author.

CHAPTER 6

Preparing Employees for Delegation

What you should expect

The manager has every right to expect results from the employee according to the parameters established when the delegation was made. Tick the expectations you feel are currently being satisfied when you delegate:

☐ 1. The employee has a willing, capable attitude and accepts responsibility for the task.

☐ 2. The employee asks questions and seeks help when needed.

☐ 3. Progress reports are provided on time to you and to others in the communications loop.

☐ 4. The finished tasks are good examples of completed staff work.

☐ 5. The employee uses initiative, and shows dedication and commitment to the task.

☐ 6. Time, money, equipment and manpower are seen as expensive resources and used accordingly.

If these expectations are to be met, the employee must be prepared in advance, permitted to grow as the work is done, and continuously developed for more difficult assignments in the future.

Preparation begins with employment

If a manager is to have a strong team of employees to whom he or she can delegate, they must be employed with that thought in mind. Human resources are the most critical part of any manager's success. Good people help ensure profitability, productivity, growth and long-term survival. Some critical elements in employee selection and placement are listed below. Indicate how well you perform by ticking the appropriate box.

	Do well	Should improve
1. I analyse job requirements thoroughly before beginning the selection process.	☐	☐
2. I always probe for objective evidence of a candidate's skills; knowledge; past successes and failures; dependability; and attitude towards work, colleagues, supervisors and customers.	☐	☐
3. I determine the type of project and task responsibility the applicant has had in previous positions, and how they have handled authority.	☐	☐
4. I make sure each applicant understands the job requirements and expected standards of performance.	☐	☐
5. I describe my idea of teamwork to applicants and ask them to assess how they would work under team conditions.	☐	☐
6. In making a selection decision, I evaluate facts carefully and avoid making premature conclusions or stereotyping.	☐	☐

	Do well	Should improve
7. People I hire are placed in positions where there is potential for success.	☐	☐

If the people you select to be on your team are successful, you will be successful.

Develop employees to handle complex tasks

Do you use delegation to build new employee skills and strengthen existing ones? Do you prepare people properly for assignments you wish to delegate to them? Your attitude, knowledge and approach will influence what is learned and how well it is applied. Here are some suggestions to improve the return on investment in training for all concerned.

Place a tick in any of the boxes below where you already do what is suggested. Place a cross in the box if you plan to begin this practice.

I normally:

☐ 1. Review performance against expectations with each employee, and jointly identify training that will strengthen results.

☐ 2. Listen to employees' growth objectives and support them through delegation when I can.

☐ 3. Talk in advance to employees selected for training, to emphasise the importance of the training to their job and their delegated assignments.

☐ 4. Have an employee's work covered by others while that employee is in formal training, so he or she can concentrate on what is being taught.

☐ 5. Help employees develop an action plan to apply their training to the job and to any additional assignments.

☐ 6. Ask the employees for an evaluation of the training programme and whether it would be suitable for other members of the team.

☐ 7. Delegate work to employees that allows them to apply new techniques and methods learned during training.

☐ 8. Compliment employees when they apply their newly acquired skills.

Teach employees problem-solving techniques

Many supervisors spend too much time solving problems that could be better handled by the employees they supervise. When supervisors try to solve all the problems, production is slowed down, employees become frustrated, and personal growth is limited. The supervisor ends up with less time to plan, organise, motivate and control. Delegation is more effective when the supervisor participates in problem solving only when necessary, instead of dominating it. In view of this, problem solving should be taught at every level of the organisation.

The problem-solving process should be as simple as possible while getting the job done. One basic approach is outlined below. Tick those steps that would be useful in your operation:

☐ **STEP 1–State what appears to be the problem.**
The real problem may not surface until facts have been gathered and analysed. Therefore, start with a supposition that can later be confirmed or corrected.

☐ **STEP 2–Gather facts, feelings and opinions.**
What happened? Where, when and how did it occur? What is its size, scope and severity? Who and what is affected? Is it likely to happen again? Does it need to be corrected? Time and expense may require problem solvers to think through what they need, and assign priorities to the more critical elements.

☐ **STEP 3–Restate the problem.**
The facts help make this possible and provide supporting data. The actual problem may or may not be the same as stated in Step 1.

☐ **STEP 4–Identify alternative solutions.**
Generate ideas. Do not eliminate any possible solutions until several have been discussed.

☐ **STEP 5–Evaluate alternatives.**
Which will provide the optimum solution? What are the risks? Are the costs in keeping with the benefits? Will the solution create new problems?

☐ **STEP 6–Implement the decision.**
Who has to be involved? To what extent? How, when and where? Who will the decision affect? What might go wrong? How will results be reported and checked?

☐ **STEP 7–Evaluate the results.**
Test the solution against the desired results. Modify the solution if better results are needed.

Make employee commitment possible

Managers cannot do everything, no matter how talented and committed they may be. Their success is measured by their ability to delegate intelligently and then motivate employees to accomplish the goals of the organisation. The highest level of achievement is attained when a team is committed to the task and full use is made of each member's talents.

Commitment cannot be forced. It is self-generating and usually develops through a feeling of involvement. People increase commitment to a team when they are allowed to contribute to its success. Once a person is actively involved in delegated projects and activities, including problem solving, a sense of ownership is developed. People feel more important and needed when they share a responsibility for results. Employees contribute their best to problem solving when they have a personal stake in doing so.

> A manager controls the degree to which employees
> are involved. Open up opportunities for participation
> through delegation, and watch the commitment grow.

Differences between delegators

The manager's attitude towards employees and their ability to
handle delegated assignments can make a significant
difference. In the two lists below, tick those items that best
describe you.

Success-centred delegator	Doubt-centred delegator
☐ Concentrates on successful results and high goals.	☐ Focuses on and transmits fear of failure. Sets fail-safe goals.
☐ Reinforces the employee's strengths and abilities. Confident of success.	☐ Expresses grave doubts about the employee's ability and limits, or reduces authority arbitrarily.
☐ Encourages employee participation in setting goals and objectives.	☐ Personally sets arbitrary goals and objectives.
☐ Readily accepts new ideas and creative solutions.	☐ Discourages anything new or untried.
☐ Communicates freely and openly. Nothing is held back.	☐ Witholds information to force the employee to ask for help.
☐ Recognises achievement and reinforces it.	

Success-centred delegator	Doubt-centred delegator
☐ Looks at the implications of each assignment for the future and assigns tasks accordingly.	☐ Doesn't recognise success until it is endorsed from above.
☐ Encourages employees to appraise their performance and suggest improvements.	☐ Focuses on short-term goals and discourages employees who see implications for the future.
	☐ Tells employees what went wrong and what to do about it.

Case Study 5
The delegation disaster

When Jim took over the systems group in the electronics division, he made up his mind to change the environment and the attitudes of the employees. His predecessor had not been an effective delegator or communicator. The employees had had little to do in a department where the supervisor was totally swamped.

Jim immediately began to delegate assignments (at fairly high authority levels) that his predecessor had performed herself. He was surprised at the results.

His employees seemed to think he was pushing *his* work on to them. Most of them complained they were neither trained nor paid to do the assignments delegated. It was not unusual for them to bring problems arising from their normal assignments to Jim for solutions, and they did not understand his saying, 'Don't bring me problems, bring me solutions.'

Has Jim overlooked anything in his approach to turning this situation around? Make your comments in the space on the following page.

Jim's delegation would have been more successful if:

_____

_____

_____

_____

_____

_____

_____

_____

_____

See page 70 for the author's comments.

CHAPTER 7

Potential Delegation Problems and How to Handle Them

Delegator's trouble-shooting guide

Possible problems	Possible solutions
1. Supervisor delegates only meaningless chores.	Delegating only meaningless chores creates resentment. Mix in some of your favourite tasks and share the more enjoyable work.
2. Employees resist the work, claiming they don't know how to do it.	Provide training as necessary, or break down the job and let them handle as many components as they can. Add more as they learn.
3. The employee says he or she is too busy.	If that is true, consider giving the task to someone else, but check their work-load first.
4. The task is repetitive, but it would take you longer to delegate the job than to do it yourself.	Get smart. At least get someone to start to learn the process. Soon they will be doing it all. Otherwise you will still be doing it next year.

Possible problems	Possible solutions
5. 'Higher management requires me to sign these invoices and other basic documents like shipping and receiving papers.'	Ask management to change the policy so that employees closer to the work can sign. You're probably already taking their word that it's all right to do so.
6. 'Poor results on this project will make me look bad.'	Your job is to let subordinates develop by taking on new endeavours. They may make some mistakes, but they will learn from them. You can minimise serious mistakes by using an appropriate level of delegation.
7. 'If my employees can do the tough jobs well, I'm not needed.'	Management desperately needs managers who can get superior performance from employees. Keep up the good work!
8. 'My supervisor expects me to do this personally.'	If that is the actual case, you had better do it, but first check up with the boss. She or he may simply want to be sure that you see the job gets done.
9. 'I'll lose my skills if I delegate too much of the work.'	Managers need to learn to manage. They need to teach their employees the skills needed for what they used to do.

Possible problems	Possible solutions
10. 'If I delegate all my work, I won't have anything to do.'	Direct your attention to planning, organising, motivating and controlling.
11. 'I don't understand the work well enough to control it or make a judgement about how well it is being done.'	Learn enough about unfamiliar areas to ask the right questions and assess the answers.
12. Employees with delegated tasks keep coming back for advice and help.	Whenever an employee asks how you would do the task, turn it around and ask how she or he would do it. Reinforce correct answers warmly. If you feel sure she or he can handle the problem, or the consequences of an error are low, be unavailable. Help your employees to build confidence.
13. Some employees are overburdened and others don't have enough to do.	The supervisor is over-delegating to those who are most trusted, and failing to develop those in whom she or he lacks confidence. It is essential to balance the work and raise the confidence level by giving everyone a chance to perform.

Possible problems	Possible solutions
14. Employees do not understand organisational objectives and standards.	Tell the employees what is at stake and the purpose of the job. As often as you can, involve the employees in setting objectives and standards.
15. 'Employees don't do things the way I do.'	Concentrate on getting the right results and learn to live with differences. You may even learn something new.
16. The supervisor either delegates everything or nothing.	Study the levels of delegation described on page 46 and learn to apply them.
17. The supervisor assigns the least challenging work to the most qualified people.	Sometimes necessary, but often done because the supervisor fears mistakes. Select a level of delegation that fits the employee and the situation. Some mistakes will occur; they will provide learning experiences. It's a serious mistake to burn out your best people.
18. The supervisor and the employee have trouble agreeing on the specifics of the delegation.	Review and clarify objectives to be sure that they are understood. Delegate accordingly. Don't be nit-picking. Follow up as necessary to see that the right results are being obtained.

Possible problems	Possible solutions
19. The employee's performance is jeopardising a successful outcome.	Identify the reason and take corrective action. This might include changing the level of authority and providing more support. Acting carelessly could shatter the employee's confidence.
20. Deadlines are not being met.	Reassess objectives, standards and priorities with the employee. Identify the reasons for missed deadlines.

CHAPTER 8

Review and Commitment to the Future

Review

Answer the following true/false questions

True   False

_____ _____ 1. Most mangers excel at delegation.

_____ _____ 2. Delegation is an indispensable management skill.

_____ _____ 3. It is alright to delegate tasks you dislike.

_____ _____ 4. Delegation is essential to the development of employees and the improvement of productivity.

_____ _____ 5. Employees appreciate your intervention in their decision making.

_____ _____ 6. The list of tasks a manager cannot delegate is quite long.

_____ _____ 7. Employees dislike managers who delegate.

_____ _____ 8. As you move up, you must learn to delegate operating tasks you once performed yourself.

True   False

_____ _____   9. Delegation is one way to use and
                    reinforce creative talents.

_____ _____ 10. Managers must always keep key results
                    areas in mind when delegating.

_____ _____ 11. Delegation is a positive act and requires
                    very little thought or preparation.

_____ _____ 12. You don't really know what people can do
                    until you give them a chance under the
                    proper conditions.

_____ _____ 13. Secretaries should be restricted to word
                    processing, filing and answering phones.

_____ _____ 14. The heart of the delegation process is the
                    interaction between the supervisor and
                    employee when the assignment is
                    communicated.

_____ _____ 15. A common management mistake is
                    failing to delegate authority
                    commensurate with the task.

_____ _____ 16. The goal in delegation is the satisfactory
                    completion of the assigned task through the
                    personal efforts of those assigned to the task.

_____ _____ 17. Teaching employees to solve problems
                    helps prepare them for delegation.

_____ _____ 18. Whenever you perform a task someone
                    else could do, you keep yourself from a
                    task only you can do.

Check your answers with the author's on the next page.

Review answers

1. False. Name five in your circle of aquaintances.

2. True. If you are not delegating, you are not managing.

3. True. There is a very good chance that you will find someone who enjoys them. We usually don't do very well what we dislike.

4. True. Try it, you'll like the results.

5. False. Do you like it?

6. False. Make a list. You will be amazed how short it is (if you are honest).

7. False. Research reflects just the opposite.

8. True. If you don't, your upward progress will stop or you will burn out.

9. True. If you don't delegate, creativity will die.

10. True. Accomplishing results in key results areas is what your job is all about.

11. False. Thought and preparation assure successful delegation.

12. True. Everyone needs a chance to show what they can do.

13. False. They are usually capable of much, much more.

14. True. This is the most important connection.

15. True. Too often it is all or nothing.

16. True. Too much interference spoils the results.

17. True. It will make your life much easier.

18. True. And don't you forget it!

Ten traps to avoid

Tick those you intend to avoid

☐ 1. Thinking you can do everything yourself.

☐ 2. Failing to give employees challenging assignments with enough leeway to handle them.

☐ 3. Careless selection of an authority level when assigning a project.

☐ 4. Overlooking delegation opportunities for untried and untested employees.

☐ 5. Holding on to non-management tasks that someone else could do.

☐ 6. Too little or too much follow-up.

☐ 7. Withholding vital information pertinent to a delegated assignment.

☐ 8. Failure to recognise employee accomplishments.

☐ 9. Overburdening your best, most trusted people because you have not prepared anyone else.

☐ 10. Failing to hold a critique with an employee after the accomplishment of a major task to see what you both have learned.

A delegation checklist

The following checklist is designed to guide the manager through the delegation process.

1. Personal preparation

I have reviewed my job and analysed or identified:

_____ my duties and responsibilities
_____ key results areas
_____ objectives
_____ management tasks versus operating work
_____ the assignments I can delegate

2. Planning the delegation

I have planned the delegation and established or considered:

_____ the objectives to be accomplished
_____ completion dates
_____ standards to be met
_____ the decision making required
_____ the amount of authority to be delegated
_____ budget and other resource requirements
_____ how involved I want to be
_____ what feedback I want and when I want it
_____ the person to whom I will delegate

3. Selecting the right person

I have selected an employee after considering:

_____ to whom the work logically belongs
_____ who has the interest or the ability
_____ who will find the work challenging
_____ who the assignment will help develop
_____ who has been overlooked in the past
_____ who is best qualified
_____ who has the time
_____ who will do the best job

4. Making the delegation

When I communicate the delegation I will:

_____ describe the task and results expected
_____ agree on standards of performance and timetables
_____ determine training needs and when training will be provided
_____ state the amount and frequency of feedback I expect
_____ define parameters and resources, including budgets
_____ spell out the level of authority
_____ tell others who is in charge

5. Following through

I will follow through by:

_____ setting reasonable reporting and review schedules
_____ respecting the level of delegation given
_____ communicating freely and openly
_____ supporting the employee to the extent required
_____ offering encouragement and reinforcing employee strengths and abilities
_____ recognising achievement
_____ intervening only if *absolutely* necessary

Develop a personal action plan

Think over the material you have read. Review the self-analysis questionnaires and the 'missed opportunities' page. Rethink the case studies and the reinforcement exercises. What have you learned about delegation? What have you learned about yourself as a delegator? How can you apply what you have learned? Make a commitment to yourself to become a better delegator and a more effective manager by designing a personal action plan to help you accomplish this goal.

The following guide may help you clarify your goals and outline the actions required to achieve them.

1. My current delegation skills are effective in the following areas:

   _____

   _____

2. I need to improve my delegation skills in the following areas:

   _____

   _____

3. My goals for improving my delegation skills are as follows (be sure they are specific, attainable and measurable):

   _____

   _____

4. These people are resources who can help me achieve my goals:

   _____

   _____

5. The following is my action plan, along with a timetable to accomplish each goal:

   _____

   _____

Responses to case studies

Case Study 1
The do-it-yourself manager

Joanne's supervisor didn't waste time getting to the point. She simply asked her to talk about her work-load and that of her subordinates. The contrast made the problem obvious. When Joanne explained her rationale, the supervisor was not convinced. She suggested that Joanne should take a good look at her subordinates and their past work record. Most were high achievers when given the chance. She suggested that Joanne was afraid to let go of responsibility and authority, and perhaps enjoyed 'doing' work more than 'managing' work. Joanne then admitted that perhaps she didn't know how to let go and still maintain control. The discussion concluded with Joanne agreeing to attend a seminar on delegating and to work closely with her supervisor when she was unsure of how to proceed.

Case Study 2:
Baffled by the budget

Jack has to release total control of the budget process in his unit in order to get operating control. He should make key staff members responsible for their part of the budget and hold them accountable for results. This means they should participate in the development of the budget and its day-to-day administration.

Jack's administrative assistant could be assigned responsibility for pulling the tentative budget together, with the help and input of the section heads. When they feel it is complete, they can present it to Jack for review and approval, and then follow up to see that everyone stays on course.

Case Study 3:
Making choices

It is good that Susan has identified Mary Wong's strengths and is delegating to her. However, she may be delegating so

69

much that Mary is carrying an unfair share of the load and other employees are being prevented from learning new things. Balancing tasks between employees is always difficult, especially when there are one or two you know can do it all. You can minimise the risk when assigning work to employees you don't know well by planning the delegation carefully, following up on progress frequently, and training as necessary. Otherwise, you and your 'Mary Wongs' will be doing all the important and complex work yourselves and your other employees will be stagnating.

Case Study 4:

The incomplete data dilemma

Like many managers, Kate is delegating sufficient authority to capable people to get the work done. Unfortunately, she is not making it clear to everyone involved who is in charge of the investigations, and much of the data input is to her instead of to the employee in charge of the project. In spite of her efforts to translate the information and pass it on quickly, she has become a communications block. Her 'translations' may not be accurate, and her intervention prevents the employee who needs the data from asking clarifying questions or requesting additional information. Her employees become defensive when she criticises them for not handling information well because she is the reason and they are reluctant to say so.

Case Study 5:

The delegation disaster

Jim is to be commended for realising the need to delegate, but he moved too quickly and without preparing his staff properly.

Instead, Jim should have taken the time to get to know each person and to learn something about their needs, abilities and goals. It would also have been helpful to share his management style and personal goals for the organisation. A gradual increase in delegated tasks with employees participating in determining the authority level would have been less threatening to the employees, since they did not seem to seem to understand delegation or have confidence in their ability to undertake new assignments.

Further Reading from Kogan Page

Develop your Management Potential: A Self-Help Guide,
  C Chambers, J Coopey and A McLean

Don't Do. Delegate!, J M Jenks and J M Kelly

The First Time Manager, M J Morris

How to be an Even Better Manager, (3rd ed), Michael Armstrong

How to Develop your Personal Management Skills, Jane Allan

How to get More Done, John and Fiona Humphrey

Better Management Skills

Effective Employee Participation, Lynn Tylczak

The Fifty-Minute Supervisor, Elwood N Chapman

How to Communicate Effectively, Bert Decker

How to Motivate People, Twyla Dell

Improving Relations at Work, Elwood N Chapman

Leadership Skills for Women, Marilyn Manning and Patricia
  Haddrock

Making an Impact in Your New Job, Elwood N Chapman

Team Building, Robert B Maddux